My First

How Living

Book of Nature
Things Grow

by Dwight Kuhn

Cartwheel
·B·O·O·K·S·™

SCHOLASTIC INC.
New York   Toronto   London   Auckland   Sydney

To my niece Joanne,
who is curious about how things grow
—D.K.

Acknowledgments: Thanks go to my wife Kathy and agent
Neil Soderstrom for their editorial help in the preparation
of this book. At Scholastic, my thanks go to Edie Weinberg,
Grace Maccarone, Bernette Ford, John Simko, Jean Marzollo,
Mark Freiman, and Emily Sper.

All photographs by Dwight Kuhn except the following: Ikan/PETER ARNOLD (29 left); Dr. Paul A.
Zahl/PHOTO RESEARCHERS, INC. (29 right); J. Cancalosi/DRK PHOTO (42 bottom, 43 bottom);
Stephen J. Krasemann/DRK PHOTO (42 top, 43 top, 54 top and bottom right, 55 bottom right); Steve
Maslowski/PHOTO RESEARCHERS, INC. (46 top); Wayne Lynch/DRK PHOTO (front cover
bottom left, 54 bottom left); Jeff Foott (55 top); Doug Perrine/DRK PHOTO (55 bottom left); Peter Veit/
DRK PHOTO (56, 57); Richard Hutchings (front cover bottom right, 58, 59, 60, 61).

Library of Congress Cataloging-in-Publication Data

Kuhn Dwight,
    My first book of nature / by Dwight R. Kuhn.
      p.   cm.—(Cartwheel learning bookshelf)
    "Cartwheel Books"—T.p. verso.
    Summary: Provides an introduction to growth, explaining how it occurs in such everyday things as
guppies, apples, dogs, trees, and humans.
    ISBN 0-590-45502-8
    1. Growth—Juvenile literature. [1. Growth.] I. Title. II. Series.
QH511.K84 1993
574.3′1—dc20   92-14329
                                                      CIP
                                                      AC

12 11 10 9 8 7 6 5 4 3 2 1   3 4 5 6 7 8/9
Printed in the U.S.A.   37
First Scholastic printing, March 1993

Introduction

From birds that soar in the air to fish that swim in the sea, all living things grow. Mushrooms pop up in the damp earth after it rains. Seeds sprout roots and stems and grow into trees that bear flowers and fruit. Caterpillars become beautiful butterflies. Ducklings peck through their egg shells, wet and tired, but before long they are gliding smoothly over the water.

Mammals such as cats, elephants, and humans need more time to grow up. Kittens practice hunting. Young elephants have play fights. Human babies need their parents for many years while they learn to walk and talk and think for themselves.

Here are 30 living things that take different paths from birth to maturity. Look at the bright, beautiful pictures and see how they grow!

Contents

Mushrooms

Mushrooms come in many different sizes, shapes, and colors. Some mushrooms grow on dead trees. Some grow among dead plants. Other mushrooms, like these shown here, grow in grassy areas. A mushroom is a kind of plant called a fungus.

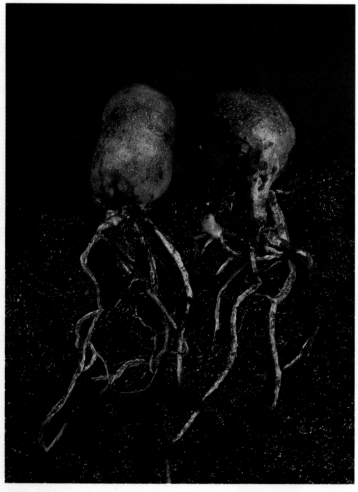

Mushrooms begin growing underground as thin rootlike threads. They cannot make their own food. Mushrooms get their food from dead leaves and other decaying matter. In time, small mushroom buttons push up out of the ground.

Like magic, mushrooms seem to pop up after a good rain. The mushroom buttons take in water and swell. Before long, the mushrooms form stalks and caps.

The cap is like an umbrella. Underneath are ridges called gills.

Inside the gills, millions of tiny spores form. New mushrooms grow from these spores. One mushroom can produce millions of spores.

Grasses

There are many different kinds of grasses. Some grow in yards, in playgrounds, and along roadsides. Grasses in farm fields include oats, wheat, and rice.

All grass needs sunlight and air to grow. It also needs the minerals and water its roots get from soil.

When grass grows tall enough, it makes delicate flowers like these. The flowers make seeds. The seeds of oats, wheat, and rice are used as foods for people and animals.

Seeds that fall onto soil start growing when the soil becomes moist and warm from the heat of the sun. They grow into new grass plants.

Dandelions

Dandelions seem to grow almost everywhere. They grow in lawns, in fields, along roadsides, and even in the narrow cracks of city sidewalks.

A dandelion plant has deep roots. Its leaves grow close to the ground. At first, dandelion flowers are bright yellow.

Then the flowers change into fluffy white seed balls. The seed balls have many seeds that blow away with the wind. Each seed has a little parachute.

The parachutes help the seeds float to new lawns, fields, and roadsides. So every year dandelions pop up in different places even though no one planted them.

Potatoes

Most people like to eat potatoes in one form or another — mashed potatoes, baked potatoes, French fries, and potato chips. Potato plants grow in a very interesting way.

Potatoes have tiny sprouts called eyes. The eyes are like seeds. They can sprout into little stems and roots. Potato farmers cut the potatoes into pieces, each with an eye. These pieces are planted in the ground.

The stems and leaves grow upward from the eye. The roots grow downward from the eye.

A potato field looks like this — all stems, leaves, and flowers. But where are the potatoes?

The potatoes grow underground. They store extra food the plant makes. By the end of summer, potatoes are big enough to be dug up and eaten. Some of the potatoes will be saved, cut up, and planted. These will grow into new potato plants.

Apple Trees

Ripe apples finish growing in late summer and early fall. Many ripe apples are red. But some are yellow, and others are green. Most apples are juicy and delicious.

An apple is the fruit of the apple tree. Inside the apple are dark brown seeds.

Apple seeds that fall to the ground may sprout in warm spring soil. The new seed-lings need sunlight, air, water, and soil in order to grow.

A mature apple tree blossoms every spring.

 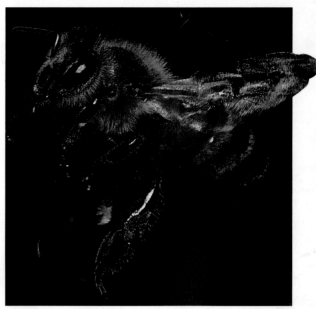

The flower blossoms have the parts needed to make apples. Bees like to visit apple blossoms. They drink a juice called nectar from the flowers. As they sip, they rub against yellow pollen from the flower. The pollen sticks to the bee. When the bee flies to another flower, it carries pollen. The pollen rubs off on the new flower and helps the new flower make seeds.

The petals fall off. Then the center part of the flower grows larger and larger. It slowly becomes an apple. The small seeds grow inside.

By the end of the summer, the apple is fully grown—ready to eat. New apple trees may grow from the seeds.

Earthworms

Earthworms are slimy, squirmy animals that live in soil. They are important animals. Earthworms help plants grow by improving the soil. They are also eaten by birds and other animals.

Earthworms push their way through the soil. As they move, they eat soil containing small pieces of dead plants and animals.

An adult earthworm makes about 20 egg cases each year. These egg cases are called cocoons. Each tiny, rubbery cocoon holds a few eggs. Within a few weeks, tiny baby worms hatch. They are ready to gobble soil, just like their parents.

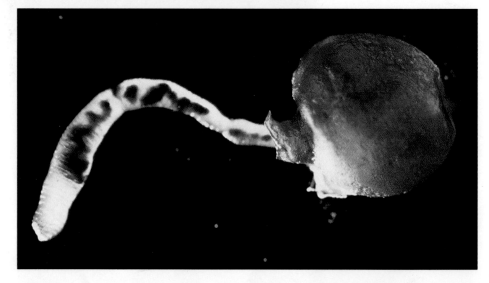

Crayfish

Crayfish are not fish. They belong to an animal family called crustaceans. Crayfish live on the bottoms of ponds, lakes, and streams. They are sometimes called mud bugs, crawdads, crawfish, or freshwater lobsters. Crayfish walk equally well in all directions — forward, backward, and sideways. When afraid, crayfish dart backward through the water with a quick flap of the tail.

The female crayfish carries her eggs around with her. She can carry 10 to 200 eggs safely under her tail.

After the eggs hatch, the babies cling to the underside of their mother's tail. When large enough, the young swim away. But they need to swim away quickly — or else their mother will eat them!

Spiders

Many people think spiders are insects. They are not. Insects have six legs. Spiders have eight.

The female garden spider lays her eggs and spins a silk egg sac around them. This egg sac protects the eggs from cold, heat, wind, and rain.

When baby spiders first hatch, they remain in the egg case. Their bodies are not completely formed. They cannot even see or move. Before long, the tiny spiders have grown enough to leave the egg case. Then they begin looking for food.

Garden spiders spin large circular webs. The webs trap insects that fly or jump into the sticky silken threads.

This spider just caught a grasshopper in its web. The spider bites the grasshopper to weaken it and wraps it in silk. Later the spider will feed on the grasshopper.

Butterflies

Butterflies are insects. They fly from flower to flower. They drink flower nectar with their long "tongues."

The female monarch butterfly lays her eggs on a milkweed plant. No other plant will do.

The monarch butterfly egg is the size of a pinhead. Here it is shown enlarged many times.

A caterpillar hatches from the egg. A caterpillar spends most of its time eating leaves. It grows quickly. After about 2 weeks, the caterpillar is fully grown.

One day the caterpillar turns into a pupa.
It forms a hard protective shell around its
body.

Inside the pupa, the caterpillar slowly
changes. It grows colorful wings and
becomes a butterfly.

The shell splits open, and a butterfly
crawls out. The butterfly holds on to the
old shell while its wings are drying. In a
few hours, the butterfly flies away.

Ladybugs

Ladybugs have a tricky name. First, they aren't all ladies — about half of them are males. Second, ladybugs are not really bugs. Ladybugs belong to a group of insects called beetles. Scientists classify bugs and beetles as two different kinds of insects. Farmers and gardeners like ladybugs because they eat insects that harm plants.

A female ladybug lays a batch of yellow eggs on a leaf.

An egg hatches into a larva. A ladybug larva eats insects called aphids. A single larva can eat 50 aphids every day.

When a larva is fully grown, it changes into a pupa. Inside the pupa, the larva slowly changes into an adult ladybug.

In a few weeks, the adult ladybug crawls out of the pupa's skin. At first, the ladybug's outer wings are yellow.

Soon the yellow wings grow hard and turn red with black spots.

Mosquitoes

Mosquitoes are insects; they have six legs. Only the female mosquito sucks blood. She is so light, she can land on a person without his knowing it. Then she sucks blood until she is full. The mosquito flies off, leaving the person with an itchy red spot.

Some mosquitoes lay a raft of eggs on top of water.

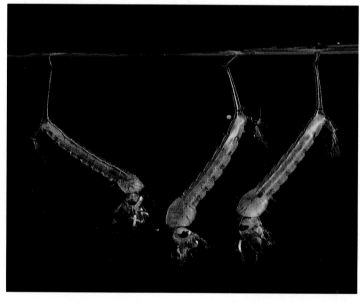

In a few days, a larva slides out of the bottom of each egg. The larva's head points down. But the larva breathes air through a tube that goes up to the surface of the water. It eats tiny food found underwater.

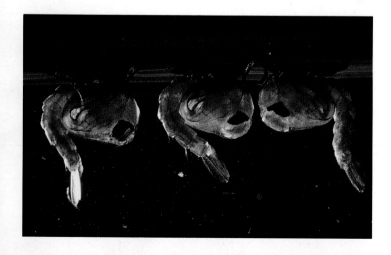

After a few weeks, the larva forms a pupa. The pupa does not eat. But it can move around in the water.

In a few days, the pupa's skin splits open.
Out comes an adult mosquito.

Here a female mosquito is sucking blood from a person's finger. She may have
hundreds of eggs inside her. Most female mosquitoes need a meal of blood to help
the eggs grow. The male mosquito feeds on plant juices instead.

Stickleback Fish

In spring, the male stickleback is very busy. He finds a place in a stream with a sandy bottom, builds a nest, and cares for the eggs and young.

The male stickleback uses water plants to build the nest.

A female stickleback enters the nest. There she lays about 50 eggs. The father waits nearby. The mother fish may eat the eggs, so the father chases her away.

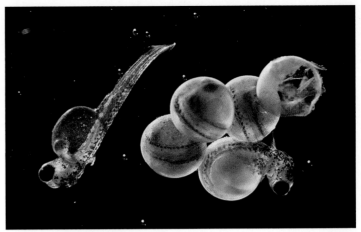

The father guards the eggs until they hatch. He uses his fins to fan water toward the nest. This brings a good supply of oxygen to the eggs.

Each newly hatched baby has a bubble-like yolk sac attached to its body. The yolk sac contains food for the baby.

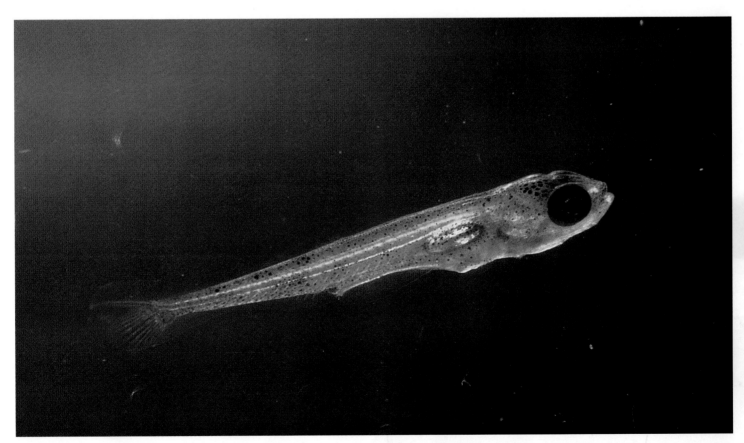

When the yolk sacs are gone, the babies find their own food. The father protects the babies from other fish as long as they stay near the nest. When the young sticklebacks are large enough, they swim away.

Guppies

Many pet stores sell guppies. These fish do not lay eggs. Baby guppies are born alive.

This photo shows a baby guppy being born. The baby has just popped out of its mother.

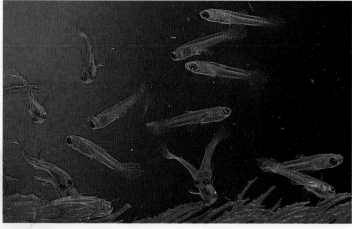

Newborn guppies know how to swim as soon as they are born. They also know how to eat tiny plants and animals in the water. They don't need their parents to care for them.

Fully grown male guppies are more colorful than females. Males usually have fancy fins and bright colors.

Seahorses

Seahorses are not really horses. They are fish that live in the sea. The seahorse gets its name from its horse-like face. The male seahorse has a pouch like a kangaroo.

The mother seahorse lays eggs in the father's pouch. Then she swims away. The father carries the eggs in his pouch for about a month. This picture shows baby seahorses being born from their father's pouch. The father squeezes his pouch until about 100 babies come out.

Baby seahorses hold onto things with their tails. They eat thousands of tiny creatures each day. Some of the baby seahorses become food for other creatures. The baby seahorses that survive to adulthood will be fathers and mothers, too.

Frogs

Frogs, salamanders, and toads are called amphibians. Most amphibians live the first part of their lives in water. When they become adults, they can live on land. These photos show how a wood frog grows.

Female wood frogs come to water to lay their eggs. The eggs are covered with a clear jelly. The eggs soon become tiny tadpoles.

Tadpoles live in water. They breathe with gills, just like fish. At first, a tadpole has a long tail. Then the tadpole grows two back legs. Next it grows two front legs as its tail becomes smaller.

Now lungs are growing inside the tadpole's body. Lungs allow the tadpole to breathe air when it climbs out of water.

Finally the tadpole's body absorbs the tail, and the tadpole becomes a frog. A frog can breathe air and live on land. Fully grown frogs jump and hop. They flick out their sticky tongues to catch insects.

Turtles

Turtles, lizards, and snakes are known as reptiles. Reptiles have dry scaly skin. The body temperature of reptiles changes with the temperature of their surroundings. On cold days, reptiles are cold. On warm days, reptiles are warm.

Turtles hatch from eggs. The eggs are soft and tough like leather. The female snapping turtle lays eggs in a sandy place.

Tiny turtles hatch in about three months. A baby turtle opens its egg with an egg tooth at the end of its beak.

The baby turtle is born with a shell.
As the turtle grows, the shell grows, too.
When in danger, the turtle pulls inside
its protective shell.

Snapping turtles are usually found in water. Some very
old snapping turtles weigh more than 60 pounds (27 kg),
about the weight of a 7-year-old child.

Snakes

A green snake is hard to see in green grass. Some snakes are hard to see because their skin colors match the grass and trees around them. Other snakes are easy to see because of the colorful patterns on their skin.

Some snakes are born alive. Others hatch from eggs. These six eggs were laid by a female green snake.

When a baby snake is ready to hatch, it pokes its head through the leathery shell.

As a snake grows, it becomes too large for its skin. So it grows shiny new skin under the old skin. The snake sheds its old skin by wiggling out and leaving it behind.

Green snakes eat insects and spiders. A snake's tongue moves in and out as it searches for food. The tongue helps the snake smell food as well as other animals.

Robins

Robins are familiar birds. Male and female robins look very much alike. But you can tell them apart if you look closely. Males have a darker head and a brighter orange breast.

Robins build a strong nest of grass, twigs, and mud for their small blue eggs.

The parents catch worms and insects to feed the babies. The hungry babies open their mouths wide whenever a parent arrives.

The parents take turns sitting on the eggs to keep them warm. The eggs need to be warm so the babies inside can grow and hatch.

The baby birds grow feathers and practice flapping their wings. Young robins need to practice before they can fly well. On their first flight, they usually just flutter to the ground. Young birds found on the ground are seldom alone. The parents are usually nearby, watching and caring for them.

Robins hop around the yard looking for juicy worms to eat.

Woodpeckers

Flickers are a kind of woodpecker. Woodpeckers peck at trees to find insects to eat. They also use their sharp beaks to hollow out nest holes in trees.

A baby flicker has no feathers when it hatches. The white point at the end of its beak is called an egg tooth. The baby uses its egg tooth to break out of the egg.

These babies can't see yet. When they hear a parent arrive with food, they open their beaks. The mother and father take turns feeding mashed insects to their babies.

The flickers are now 2 weeks old. They are beginning to climb around inside the nest hole. Their feathers are short and stubby.

This 3-week-old flicker peeks out of the nest. Soon it will learn to fly from the nest and hunt insects on its own.

Ducks

Some ducks are wild and stay away from people. Other ducks are raised by people. These photographs show how a barnyard duck grows.

A mother duck lays her eggs in a nest. She sits on them to keep them warm.

In a few hours, the ducklings' feathers are fluffy and dry.

After 28 days, a duckling pecks through the eggshell with its egg tooth. As the eggshell cracks open, a wet baby duckling pushes its way out.

Young ducklings are good swimmers. They use their webbed feet to paddle through the water. They like to stay together.

These ducklings are just 17 days old. They have grown quickly. White feathers are beginning to appear.

The yellow ducklings grow into beautiful white adult ducks.

Kangaroos

Kangaroos come in many sizes. The red and the gray kangaroos stand taller than most people. Other kinds are as small as rats. Kangaroos are mammals called marsupials. Opossums and koalas are marsupials, too.

In one way, marsupials are different from other mammals. The mother carries the baby in a special pouch on her belly. The tallest kangaroo in this picture is a mother. She has a baby growing inside her pouch.

At first the newborn kangaroo is about the size of a bean. Moments after birth, the baby crawls across its mother's belly to her pouch and begins nursing. After 6 months, the young kangaroo leaves the pouch. For the next few months, it jumps back into the pouch whenever it is frightened or needs to eat and rest. Young kangaroos are called joeys.

Joeys soon learn to use their strong hind legs to jump. Their long tails help them keep their balance. Larger kangaroos can leap 25 feet (8 m) in a single jump.

A kangaroo rests by leaning on its tail.

Mice

Mice are mammals. Mother mammals nurse their babies with milk from their bodies. Some other mammals are kangaroos, raccoons, cats, dogs, horses, elephants, dolphins, gorillas, and humans.

These mice are just 1 day old. They are born without fur. They can't see because their eyes haven't opened yet.

A mother white-footed mouse cuddles next to her babies to keep them warm. She nurses them and cleans them with her tongue.

Young white-footed mice leave their nest when they are about 1 month old. Their fur is gray. They eat berries, insects, nuts, and seeds.

Fully grown white-footed mice have reddish-brown fur. Big eyes help them see well at night. Big ears help them hear enemies. Long whiskers help them feel their way around.

Raccoons

A young raccoon is easy to recognize. It looks almost like its parents. All raccoons have a black-ringed tail and a black mask.

In spring, a mother raccoon has several fuzzy little cubs. They drink their mother's milk.

Cubs learn how to catch food in water with their hands. They catch crayfish, fish, and tadpoles.

They also eat other things, such as eggs, nuts, fruits, vegetables, and small animals. They even like garbage.

Young raccoons are natural explorers. They are very curious. They like to play, hide, and climb.

Cats

Cats are popular pets. They are curious, playful, soft, and cuddly mammals.

Newborn kittens keep warm by cuddling close to their mother. Here they are drinking her milk. She cleans the kittens with her tongue.

Kittens are born with their eyes shut. They can make sounds but cannot see or hear yet.

These kittens are 16 days old. Now they can see and hear.

As kittens grow, they learn to do many things. They learn to drink milk and eat from a dish.

They play, fight, and practice hunting. They also climb, jump, sleep, and snoop inside shoes.

Dogs

There are many kinds of dogs: big dogs, little dogs, dogs with long hair, and dogs with short hair. All dogs are mammals. Dogs make great pets and can be great friends.

These tiny springer spaniel puppies are just 8 hours old. They cannot open their eyes yet. They spend most of their time eating and sleeping.

The puppies are now 3 weeks old. Their eyes are open, and they are learning to walk.

As the puppies grow, they wrestle and chase each other. Their play helps them grow strong.

This mother is one of the puppies in the other photos. Now she has grown up. She feeds her own puppies and keeps them safe and warm, just as her mother did.

Horses

Horses are strong, graceful mammals. Cowboys and some police officers may ride them at work. Other people ride horses just for fun.

A baby horse has been growing inside this mare for 11 months. The mare will soon give birth to a baby called a foal.

After the foal is born, the mother licks and nuzzles it.

Within an hour, the foal tries to stand up. Its legs are weak and wobbly. Each time the foal tries to stand, its leg muscles become stronger. In a few hours, the foal can run and jump.

For 6 months, the foal drinks its mother's milk. It also eats grass, grain, and hay.

The foal likes to play with other young horses. It learns to gallop faster and faster. When a female horse is 4 years old, she can have a baby of her own.

Elephants

Elephants are the largest animals on land. An adult elephant might be 10 feet tall (3 m) and weigh 12,000 pounds (5,455 kg). The long trunk is much more than a nose for breathing and smelling. It also allows the elephant to eat and drink. With its trunk, the elephant slurps up water to squirt into its mouth. The elephant also uses its trunk to gather grass and leaves to eat. An adult elephant can eat 300 pounds (136 kg) of food every day.

A baby grows inside its mother for 22 months before being born. A newborn stands about 3 feet (91 cm) tall. The mother nurses the baby and takes good care of it.

Young elephants play, splash in water, and practice fighting. They like to roll in dirt and mud. Males and females grow white tusks to help them plow the ground to find roots to eat. The tusks are also used as weapons.

Females and young elephants group together in a herd. All females help watch over and protect the babies.

Dolphins

Most dolphins live in the ocean. They may look like fish, but dolphins are mammals. Fish can get oxygen from water; dolphins need to go to the surface for air. Dolphins are very smart. They use many different sounds to talk to one another.

The baby is born tail first. It swims close to its mother. Like all mammals, a dolphin baby drinks milk from its mother's body. The baby nurses for about a year and then begins eating fish.

Most young dolphins stay with their mothers for 2 to 6 years. The mothers teach them what they need to know to survive.

Dolphins swim to the surface to breathe. A dolphin has a breathing hole, called a blowhole, on top of its head. The hole closes when the dolphin dives underwater.

Gorillas

Gorillas live in dense forests in Africa. A big male stands 6 feet (183 cm) tall and can weigh 400 pounds (182 kg). Most of the time gorillas are gentle mammals.

The female gorilla normally gives birth to one baby. She holds the baby gently as she nurses it. A newborn clings to its mother's chest. As the baby grows stronger, it rides on her back. Baby gorillas learn to crawl at 2 months and walk at 8 months.

Young gorillas act a lot like human children. They like to play. They wrestle, climb trees, and slide down branches.

The young gorillas become part of a small group. The oldest and biggest male is usually the group's leader. He is called a *silverback* because he has silver hair on his back. The other gorillas follow him as he wanders in search of food.

Humans

The world has billions of people. In some ways, we are all different. Some are old. Some are young. Some are male. Some are female. People come in different sizes, shapes, and colors. But in other ways, people are the same. We are all mammals. We are born and grow in the same way. And we all need food, water, air, shelter, and love.

A human baby grows for 9 months inside its mother's body. There the baby is warm and safe.

For the first few months, the baby cries, eats, and sleeps. She needs someone to take care of her.

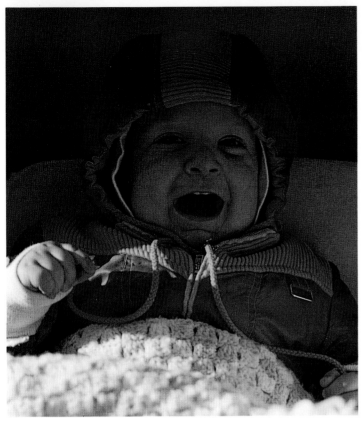

As the baby grows, he learns to recognize many things. He smiles when he hears his parents' voices and when he sees friendly faces. He learns to hold things, roll over, and crawl.

When he is about 1 year old, the baby learns to walk, talk, and play with toys.

As children grow, they learn to do things on their own.

Children also learn how to play with others. They learn how to share, take turns, and resolve fights. Children learn many things from parents, friends, teachers, and other grown-ups.

As children become teenagers, their bodies change. Teenagers are young men and women.

A man and woman can make a baby. It takes many years for human parents to raise their young.

As people grow older, their bodies continue to change. And they still continue to learn many things.